HEIFETZ *Collection*

HAVANAISE
for Violin and Piano

CAMILLE SAINT-SAËNS, Op. 83

Critical Urtext Edition
Violin Part

Edited by Endre Granat

KEISER

HAVANAISE
for Violin and Piano

Violin

Critical Urtext Edition
Edited by Endre Granat

CAMILLE SAINT-SAËNS, Op. 83

Copyright © 2015 The Jascha Heifetz Estate
Sole selling agent Lauren Keiser Music Publishing (ASCAP).
International Copyright Secured. All rights reserved.

Violin

1) Bowings by Jascha Heifetz

2) Bowings Jascha Heifetz

3) Jascha Heifetz   4) Jascha Heifetz

5) Tempo by Jascha Heifetz

NEW PUBLICATIONS FOR VIOLIN

The HEIFETZ Collection

We are pleased to introduce an exclusive series of Jascha Heifetz violin editions including wonderful and yet previously unpublished arrangements and transcriptions from Heifetz's own manuscripts.

G.F. HANDEL
PASSACAGLIA FOR TWO VIOLINS

Ed. Stephen Shipps/ Endre Granat Outside of his native Norway, Johan Halvorsen (1864-1935) is known internationally only for his arrangement of Handel's Harpsichord Suite. The Passacaglia is performed as a mainstay of Duo programs in his arrangements for both Violin/Viola and Violin/Cello. Jascha Heifetz established these duos in the standard literature by playing and recording countless performances with William Primrose and Gregor Piatigorsky. HL00126549—S512002..$22.95

CAMILLE SAINT-SAËNS
HAVANAISE FOR VIOLIN AND PIANO

Ed. Endre Granat. The Havanaise (Habanera in French) by Camille Saint-Saëns op.83 dates from 1885-87. The composer dedicated this work to Rafael Diaz Albertini, a violinist of Cuban origin. In 1888 Saint-Saëns completed the orchestration of the Havanaise . This Critical Urtext Edition is based on the composer's manuscript, the first print of the violin and piano version, and to a large part, on the historic recording by the composer himself with the violinist Gabriel Willaume (1919). HL00141932—S511022..$14.95

CAMILLE SAINT-SAËNS
INTRODUCTION AND RONDO CAPRICCIOSO OP. 28, CRITICAL URTEXT EDITION

Ed. Endre Granat. The Introduction and Rondo Capriccioso for Violin and Orchestra was originally intended to be the rousing Finale to Saint-Saëns' First Violin Concerto, op.20. Saint-Saëns' favorite violinist Pablo de Sarasate gave the first performance in 1867 in Paris with the Composer conducting. In 1869 Saint-Saëns entrusted his younger colleague Georges Bizet to create a reduction of the orchestra score for Violin and Piano. The composer's autograph score and the first edition of the work were the primary source material for this publication.
HL00141931—S511021..$14.95

HENRYK WIENIAWSKI
POLONAISE BRILLANTE NO. 1 (Polonaise de Concert)

Ed. Endre Granat. In 1848, the thirteen year old Henryk Wieniawski wrote the first sketches to his Polonaise in D major. Tremendously popular already during the composer's life time, this work has been on the repertory of virtually every virtuoso violinist ever since. This new Critical Urtext Edition corrects obvious misprints while keeping the format of the 1853 first edition, incorporating the textural the later Paris version as foot notes.
HL00141930—S511020..$12.95

HENRYK WIENIAWSKI
POLONAISE BRILLANTE NO. 2

Ed. Endre Granat. Henryk Wieniawski completed his Polonaise No. 2 at the zenith of his career in 1869. This virtuoso piece showcases the playing of many fast, short and accented notes on one bow stroke, called the Wieniawski staccato, whilte the slow midsection in F major contains some of his most lyrical themes.
HL00126550—S511019..$14.95

CONTEMPORARY SOLOS *Original works & transcriptions*

J.S. BACH—TOCCATA AND FUGUE IN D MINOR FOR SOLO VIOLIN

Arr. Stuart Carlson. Intrigued by the fact that many of the chords and motifs within Bach's famous *Toccata and Fugue* for organ could be adapted for the violin, competition-winning soloist Stuart Carlson created this virtuosic arrangement. It is in the piece's original key, and it is designed to convey the full and grand sound of the organ to the solo violin. This arrangement intentionally creates the true sound of Bach's piece, while adding variation-like figures within the Fugue's main theme. HL00124287—S510009 ....$11.95

STEPHEN HARTKE—NETSUKE FOR VIOLIN & PIANO

Netsuke are Japanese miniature carvings that were originally made to secure objects suspended from a man's sash. This piece was inspired by six exquisite carvings from the Bushell Collection at the Los Angeles County Museum of Art.
HL00042670—X511045...$37.95

YEVHEN STANKOVYCH—ANGELS' TOUCH FOR VIOLIN & PIANO

When recounting the premiere performance of *Angels' Touch,* violinist Solomiya Ivakhiv describes a work which "embodies a child-like mysticism, exploring naivety, hope, and inner peace leading to enlightenment. It is sprinkled with Ukrainian folklore elements from the Carpathian Mountains, also reminding me of my own childhood." HL00127941—S511018...$12.95

YEVHEN STANKOVYCH—CONCERTO NO. 2 FOR VIOLIN AND ORCHESTRA—SOLO/ PIANO REDUCTION

This is the first print edition of celebrated composer Yevhen Stankovych's second violin concerto, featuring cadenzas, fingerings and bowings by violinist Dima Tkachenko. Duration ca. 24' HL00141939—S511023...$24.95

Prices subject to change without notice.